THIS TIME GET IT RIGHT

Good-Bye ObamaCare;

Health Savings Accounts Open the Door to Universal Coverage and Lower Costs

Put The Patient In Charge; Melding The Conservative & Progressive

A Plan Both Republicans and Democrats Can Agree To

Henry F. Field

Thanks to family and friends, especially my wonderful wife, Beryl F. Bergen

And with hopes that my grandson, Benjamin James Jewett, has a fulfilling, loving future, full of reason and evidence

Also by Henry F. Field:

The Bumbling Colossus: The Regulatory State vs. the Citizen: How Good Intentions Fail and the Example of Health Care: A New Progressive's Guide (CreateSpace 2012, an Amazon.com company)

For advanced reading on the topics raised in **The Bumbling Colossus**, go to the **Center for Continuing Learning on the Bumbling Colossus**, at *www.thebumblingcolossus.com*

"Why There is No Individual Right to Guns", Crazy Red, *www.henryfield.blogspot.com*

Printed by IngramSpark, St. Louis, Mo.

Contents

Summary: Put the Patient In Charge

What you are about to read is the best way to get health insurance coverage to all Americans, based on progressive goals implemented by the free market. Contrary to conventional thinking, that is the only way to achieve the goal of a cost-effective universal system. It is politically unifying — satisfying the needs of Democrats and Republicans — and differs completely from what was done before.

Flush with political power in 2009 and not needing to cross the aisle, the new Obama Administration and old progressive allies in Congress forged a "top-down" bureaucratic re-structuring of the American health care system, "ObamaCare". While benefiting some, by now most people see it as largely a failure. The promises made to enable passage proved false. Costs rose unconscionably for all those unable to qualify for expanded Medicaid, and the mandated, one-size-fits-all policies narrowed choices, sometimes to nothing.

We need to replace it with something that builds on individual and family responsibility. ObamaCare did the opposite, fostering dependency on government. What we suggest here melds progressive ideals with conservative economic sense. It is simple and "bottom-up", building on an existing legal structure.

First, everyone should have a Health Savings Account (HSA), reconfigured for this purpose. HSAs are tax-free accounts which by law must be tied to so-called "catastrophic" health insurance. Overnight, doing this creates universal insurance coverage for all substantial health risks, for all. Everyone is covered. Too poor to afford it? Government steps in with credits or vouchers paid to their HSA, scaled to income, so people can buy their own coverage. Routine costs are paid from the HSA with credits or cash. Rich, poor, or somewhere in the middle, everyone has health insurance and the means to pay routine costs.

What about pre-existing conditions? Insurance is for risks, not certainties, and pre-existing conditions are known and certain. Not proper for insurance. If the public choice is made to cover them they should be in a separate pool, backed by government.

What about the 2000+ state and federal mandates and controls, most imposed by narrow special interests, which require carriers to include in all policies many items few really want. These restrict choice and drive up costs. Sweep them away with the stroke of the pen. The HSA/voucher regime, with a separate pool for pre-existing conditions, makes most unnecessary, and the free market better addresses what remains.

What about the federal health subsidy programs — Medicare, Medicaid, CHIP? Every person eligible for these should have an HSA, staged over time to replace the "top-down" bureaucracies. This way no one loses present coverage and everyone gains the benefits of free market-driven cost reduction.

Some decry the free market as "heartless" and "cruel", and cling to government control of health care. But there is nothing heartless about affording people HSAs and the resources and freedom to use them. Free markets provide special satisfactions, and rest on a compelling, poorly recognized moral basis. The HSA-based system set out here rests firmly on that moral basis, satisfies the health needs of all Americans, and fulfills the political goals of both Democrats and Republicans.

How to Replace ObamaCare

The main pieces of a replacement for ObamaCare's top-down approach follow. Moving ahead requires empowering the patient-consumer, from the "bottom-up". Only this creates a natural means to control costs – the power of markets and competition – while also ensuring that quality is enhanced. Government controlled systems – single-payer or otherwise, trap us in an insuperable dilemma, where every effort to cut costs also reduces the quality of service provided. Giving everyone the power of the purse solves this dilemma.

Goal: Health Care Should Be Universal, Accessible, and Affordable for all Americans, Without Super-Inflationary Costs

Guiding Principles:

1. Support Individual and Family Responsibility, End Bureaucratic Dependency

2. Maximize Market Features and the Power of Incentives and Competition to Lower Prices while Increasing Quality

3. Make Sure No One is Left Out

4. The Role of Government is to Help Fund the Needy, But Not Run Things. "Fund it, Don't Run it."

5. Health Care Should Not Be Free.

Solution: Return Health Care to its Roots by Building around redone Health Savings Accounts, for everyone, funded where needed by government to help provide access and choice for the poor and to deal with pre-existing conditions.

Key Elements:

1. *Universal Health Savings Accounts.* Every Individual and Family Should Have a Health Savings Account, as amended. By law, these are tied to insurance covering all "catastrophic" or substantial health risks. People choose how high a deductible and therefore premium they want. Contributions are fully tax-deductible and funds grow tax free. Premiums and routine costs are paid from the HSA.

2. *Government Funds the Needy.* Those too poor to fund their HSA receive public funding, by credits, vouchers or the equivalent, in their HSA. These are only usable with legitimate providers. Scale this down with matching grants as means increase above the poverty line.

3. *Public Support for Pre-Existing Conditions.* Insurance is to guard against risks, not certainties. Pre-existing Conditions are known and certain, therefore Not Appropriate for Insurance. Carve these items out of coverage and put them in a separate program with public support.

4. *Eliminate Most Government Mandates.* Providing everyone with HSAs and the poor with credits eliminates the need for and reason behind the over-2000 costly legislative mandates. These state (and now federal) rules require special interest-driven coverages most people would choose not to pay for, like naturopaths, drug abuse treatment, morbid obesity treatment, massage therapists, mental health. People wishing such coverage may so choose. This frees insurers to create and people to choose policies tailored to their circumstances, giving choice and vastly reducing costs.

5. *Allow Interstate Sale of Health Insurance.* No reason exists to prohibit interstate sales. Competition drives down costs. States retain supervision over the financial condition of insurers HQ'd in their state.

6. *End the Favoring of Employment–Based Plans.* Employees receive untaxed income in health benefits, and employers deduct these expenses. This has grossly distorted the market, encouraging low-deductible all inclusive plans tied to employment. A huge upward driver of costs. Deters employee job movement. Best solution – give all people the same exclusion from tax which now just employees receive.

7. *Promote Information on Choices and Costs.* People need to be able to figure out what coverage to buy. Private sources will, in time, fill the information gap. A great business opportunity for service. Government can encourage these with suitable incentives.

8. *Integrate with Medicare and Medicaid.* Age and income status do not nullify the benefits of HSAs in lower costs and expanded quality. Over time, put HSAs at the center of these programs. Make sure no one loses present coverage, replaced by an HSA.

What This Does:

It restores the American family and individual to center place in the payment for, and therefore the responsibility for, his or her own health care. It is straight-forward, complete, and unifying of all political persuasions.

Will it work? Real life proof exists in what Singapore has done over the last 35 years with its health care, achieving quality while lowering costs, based upon a system comparable to what is advanced here, discussed in chapter 6.

For more in depth, click on **www.thebumblingcolossus.com**, with current events and stories revealing themes from *The Bumbling Colossus,* by Henry F. Field (2012, amazon.com).

Outline of Topics

A. The "Old Progressives" Still Hold the Reins, but the "New Progressives" are the Future

The Old Progressive Approach

The Old Progressive Ideas Have Hit the Wall

Time for a New Progressive Approach

The New Progressive Embraces the Market

Single-Payer Systems Attract, but Destroy

B. Moving Beyond the Old Thought Framework

The New Progressive Approach to Health Care

What are the Basics?

Virtue and Well-Being in the Free Market

Why Health Care is not a Market Failure

Support Participation, Don't Cripple the Beast

C. Wash Those Dead Ideas Right Out of your Hair

Do Markets Foster Greed and Harm the Public?

The 2007-08 Crisis: The Feds Spurred it on, then Hid

Greed: Public and Private Contrasted

Public Sector Unions and Private: Beware the Rent-Seekers

D. The Merger of the New Progressive and Liberal Conservative

1

The "Old Progressive" Approach

The "Old Progressives" Still Hold the Reins, but the "New Progressives" Are the Future

1. The Old Progressive Approach; The Patient as Dependent

ObamaCare, like its 2009-10 political siblings the $787 billion "Stimulus" and the Dodd-Frank enactment to reform our financial system, derived from long-standing "old" progressive concepts. Starting with TR and Woodrow Wilson, then ballooning with FDR's "New Deal" and LBJ's "Great Society", old progressive enactments were based upon the assumption that people in economic or other distress lack suitable responsibility, or the required sense to know what is best for themselves, and experts are needed to run things and make choices for them. Markets are disparaged as favoring the rich, duping the consumer, fostering greed, and excluding the needy. Academic support for this followed, largely elaborating on "market failures" and promoting extensive government regulation of markets as the cure.

Over time, the universities and public policy schools responded and flourished, spitting out bright, fresh young graduates filled with enthusiasm and the conviction that the world needs what they have learned and them to craft it according to their learned commands. A "Government-University Complex" evolved, and huge public sums have been appropriated to their ends. Both parties have been complicit in this, although Democrats proudly crow about being in the lead. The universities, especially in the social sciences and humanities, have come to reflect an overwhelming liberal/progressive consensus, marked by

1

solidarity in an implicit belief that markets are arenas where the strong prey on the weak, requiring central government intervention.

Surprisingly, for all the noise and thunder, there has been very little light. Some programs have been relatively successful, like Social Security and Medicare/Medicaid, although design errors and demographics pose significant cost threats. Others, largely efforts to eliminate poverty, especially for inner-city minorities, have hardly budged the needle. Too many people are stuck in low-achievement, non-competitive status. High inner-city unemployment rates reflect this. Even eight years with an African-American President determined to make large-scale redistribution through structural changes to the economy achieved next to nothing to help these people. Something is amiss with the old progressive world view.

Thomas Sowell, a top-notch economist and an African American, describes the old progressives as having "The Vision of the Anointed", in a book of that name (1995). These people see problems of the world as requiring their expertise in fashioning large-scale government controls, implemented "top down" through bureaucracies filled with their like-minded, to subdue what they view as the crude and unfeeling chaos of free markets. This vision grants "a special state of grace" to its believers, an assumed moral superiority based on identification with and support for perceived victims and oppressed, and the unjustified "privileged" status of everyone else. Little supporting evidence or careful reasoning is used, in fact is scorned as the product of bias. Those who disagree "are seen as not being merely in error, but in sin..... Problems exist because others are not as wise or virtuous as the anointed":

> "This vision so permeates the media and academia, and has made such inroads into the religious community, that many grow to adulthood unaware that there is any other way of looking at things, or that *evidence* might be relevant in checking out the assumptions of so-called 'thinking people'. These might better be called '*articulate*' people, as people whose verbal nimbleness can elude both evidence and logic. This can be a fatal talent, when it

supplies the crucial insulation from reality behind many historic catastrophes."[1]

We have lived with this so long and resounded in its echoes daily so often that the essential blindness and unreality it fosters goes unnoticed. When some unexpected unmistakable event jars us into consciousness, we find it hard to grasp.

The catastrophes wrought by the "top-downers" are usually slow to unfold and, after the fact, the cause proves difficult to unravel. The New Deal is an example. Although the depression begun in 1929 was well on its way to recovery by 1933-4, it did not do so. FDR commenced in 1933, when his initial slew of market-controlling programs launched, including the Agricultural Adjustment Act and the National Recovery Administration, both of which forced up prices through combines and collaborations. As noted economists Harold Cole and Lee Ohanian put it:

> "Why wasn't the Depression followed by a vigorous recovery, like every other cycle? It should have been. The economic fundamentals that drive all recoveries were very favorable during the New Deal. [productivity growth, stable prices, low real interest rates, plentiful liquidity] ... Nobel Laureate Robert Lucas and Leon Rapping calculated just on the basis of expansionary Federal Reserve policy that the economy should have been back to normal by 1935."

> "So what stopped a blockbuster recovery from ever starting? The New Deal. Some New Deal policies ... violated the most basic economic principles by suppressing competition, and setting prices and wages in many sectors well above their normal levels. All told, these anti-market policies choked off powerful recovery forces .... Our research indicates that New Deal labor and industrial policies prolonged the Depression by seven years."[2]

Seven years is a long time to be out of work thanks to erroneously-conceived efforts to help. Perhaps the millions harmed would have preferred less empathy and solicitude and more government "hands-off".

Myth rides in the saddle while Truth walks behind. The myth that the New Deal solved the Great Depression endures today despite the fact that, at the time, it was a known failure. FDR's Treasury Secretary, Henry Morganthau, Jr., testified to Congress in 1939 that "We are spending more than ever before and it does not work. … After eight years of this Administration we have just as much unemployment as when we started. …And an enormous debt to boot."

The endurance of the New Deal myth is shown by the fact that, seventy years later, in 2009-10, Obama saw his mission as fulfilling its unfinished program. The new Obama Administration, joined by leadership in Congress, crafted its own extraordinarily prolix, confusing and impenetrably massive "top-down" government controls in two major areas of the economy: health care and banking/finance. It was so confused, by the end of Obama's eight years, many regulations and commissions supposed to be completed were still in formulation.

The result was a predictable "disaster in slow motion". As described in *The Bumbling Colossus* (amazon.com 2012), Dodd-Frank's financial reforms never addressed the basic cause of the 2007-8 implosion and just heaped extraordinary costs of regulatory compliance and uncertainty on the nation's banks, gumming up their ability to facilitate growth. A decade later, America is no safer from "too big to fail" than before, as even Larry Summers, Obama's top economics advisor during 2009-10 when Dodd-Frank was crafted, now agrees, based in part on his own studies.[3] But we are nonetheless saddled with an octopus of bureaucracy ensuring that slow growth of jobs continues, injuring the silent millions discouraged from work, until the Dodd-Frank catastrophe can be substantially repealed.[4]

And make no mistake, the harm to someone wanting a job that should but doesn't exist is hard to see but is perhaps the worst harm policymakers can inflict. No consolation that the harm is inflicted empathically with the best of intentions.

With health care, although the economy was just in early stage recovery, Obama's priority was not to grow jobs; rather, it was to achieve redistribution by restructuring the entire area of health care according to the conventional progressive design. Drafted in secret in Speaker Pelosi's chambers, ObamaCare runs to thousands of pages, and creates 159 new boards, commissions, and agencies, each to issue countless new regulations. "The Secretary" (of HHS) was specifically mentioned 1,563 times, each time empowering additional new rules. Every domain of health care was put under the federal thumb. [5]

ObamaCare perfectly exemplifies Thomas Sowell's "Vision of the Anointed". Drawing "experts" from the policy schools and old progressive think tanks, well versed in exclusive "top-down" thinking and unfamiliar with free markets and their actual operation, no one was permitted to read the thing until too late – after it passed. Arrogance combines with ignorance when The Vision is in control.

By 2016, the laughing and praise of the act's passage had long morphed into the bitter realization that the promises made were hollow, and some key ones deliberately false. As Jeff Jacoby, columnist for the Boston Globe, summarizes:

> "Obama was certain the measure would win public support, because of three promises he made over and over: that the law would extend health insurance to the 47 million uninsured, that it would significantly reduce health-insurance costs, and that Americans who had health plans or doctors they liked could keep them."

> "But Obamacare has been a fiasco. At least 27 million Americans are still without health insurance, and many of those who are newly insured have simply been added to the Medicaid rolls. Far from reducing costs, Obamacare sent premiums and deductibles skyrocketing. Insurance companies, having suffered billions of dollars in losses on the Obamacare exchanges, have pulled out from many of them, leaving consumers in much of the country with few or no options. And the administration, it transpired,

knew all along that millions of Americans would lose their medical plans once the law took effect. The deception was so egregious that in December 2013, PolitiFact dubbed "If you like your health plan, you can keep it" as its "Lie of the Year."[6]

Dodd-Frank and ObamaCare reflect the old progressive view that government, armed with good intentions and empathy, will solve all ills. But good intentions and empathy are not enough for good public policy. They can even get in the way. The test of leadership is "not in the talk but in the walk", in the acts done. What are their actual effects in real life. The media and the casual observer can survive on intentions, empathy, and oratory, but the seeker of knowledge must dive deeper.

How Good Intentions Can Create Harm

This is where economic thinking comes in — supported by a profession devoted to looking under the hood. Start with the insight that the effects of actions are not always as intended; often, quite the opposite. As Sheldon Richman notes; "In 1848, the French free market economist Frederic Bastiat taught a lesson most people still have not learned:

"In the economic sphere, an act, a habit, an institution, a law produces not only one effect, but a series of effects. Of these effects, the first alone is immediate; it appears simultaneously with its cause; *it is seen*. The other effects only emerge subsequently, *they are not seen*; we are fortunate if we *foresee* them."

"There is only one difference between a bad economist and a good one; the bad economist confines himself to the *visible* effect; the good economist takes into account both the effect that can be seen and those effects that must be foreseen." (AIER "Research Brief", June 27, 2017).

Cheering the visible effect of good intentions without careful attention to predicted secondary effects is a recipe for disaster. For example, giving to someone who asks you for money has the "first order" effect of temporarily increasing their cash resources. But when a job possibility opens, do they take it or prefer to survive on the expectation of further handouts. Examining the "second order" effects is the job of economics. This also translates to the law of unintended consequences and the theorem "there's no free lunch".

Proponents of Dodd-Frank and ObamaCare fixated on the first order effect and neglected what followed. Meanwhile, the public floats along on a false sense of reassurance thinking "the experts know better" and besides, it was all well-intended. But when the lid is lifted on these signature government interventions of 2009-10, they are revealed as harmful failures. Imagined expertise and good intentions got the laws passed but left the country burdened with a false security and unanticipated harms.

The breeding ground for the 2009-10 interventions and their popular support is the widely-held belief that the free market has failed and is the source of harms, requiring government to fix. But as shown later, the 2008 financial crisis was not the result of insufficient government but the opposite, and health care is not an arena of market failure. In both cases, the government intervention caused excessive, on-going harms.

Why were they created? The anti-market attitude reflected sits, at bottom, on an intellectual crevasse. People condemn free markets as "heartless" and cruel because they don't conform to the morality of family, tribes, or church. So they see government as savior. A problem or crisis? Do something. Pass a law which professes benefits and cures.

But this attitude is deeply flawed. As often as not, good intentions and empathy lead to harm, not the benefit promised. Is it mean-spirited, heartless and cruel to resist some program of the moment if the visible first-order effects prove weak and transitory and the second-order, invisible effects prove permanent and destructive? Calling the one heartless and the other not is upside down thinking.

Why, after trillions of dollars spent on anti-poverty programs since 1964, are so many people trapped in a cycle of unproductive life-styles and dependency, apparently in many cases because of the proliferation of government programs rather than despite them? If money, good intentions and empathy were enough, the poverty rate would be zero. Something is wrong with the old progressive assumptions and way of thought.

How did we get here and why are we stuck? Peel away the layers, and at bottom we seem trapped in a false and mistaken moral view, which created and perpetuates the politics of ever-increasing government and disparages the quite remarkable benefits of the free market. What most people think of as "moral" (self-sacrifice, particular known beneficiaries, un-self interested intention to aid) is the morality of family, church groups and tribes. We applaud those who act beneficently. But this morality can not be imposed upon the operation of free markets, which rely upon cooperation and trust, but not self-sacrifice or beneficence. To function for everyone's benefit, markets must operate on the individual buyer and seller's self-interest. Only then can markets create benefit for all. This is Adam Smith's Paradox, discussed later. It is an immutable economic law.

Old progressives deny this. And therein lies the fault. What matters for social benefit is not just good intentions and empathy, as old progressives champion, but a sympathetic understanding based upon clarity of moral reasoning and an eye to the unseen but very real results of public actions. This is the heart and soul of the best political economy, for which math and models are handmaidens.

You don't need to be an economist, but you do need some education in what the profession has learned from Adam Smith on. Some reject economic thinking because often economists disagree. This loses the forest for the trees. There is always better and worse, among economists as in all professions. In the end, superior theory, evidence and prediction win out. And there are some clear "forever" continuities. The law of supply and demand. There's no free lunch. The law of unanticipated consequences. Unseen secondary effects. The invisible hand. Those are what we rely on here. See how it unfolds.

[1] Thomas Sowell, *The Vision of the Anointed; Self-Congratulation as a Basis for Social Policy*, at 3-6 (Basic Books 1995). For the overwhelming liberal/progressive consensus in academia, see John F. Zipp & Rudy Fenwick, "Is the Academy a Liberal Hegemony", Public Opinion Quarterly, Vol 70, Issue 3 (2006); Neil Gross & Solon Simmons, "The Social and Political Views of American Professors", Harvard U. working paper Sept 24, 2007.

[2] Harold Cole and Lee Ohanian, "New Deal Policies and the Persistence of the Great Depression; A General Equilibrium Analysis", Federal Reserve Bank of Minneapolis Working Paper 597 (May 2001). The quote is from Harold Cole and Lee Ohanian, "How Government Prolonged the Depression," 2/2/2009 *WSJ*. The Henry Morganthau, Jr. quote is in Professor Burton Folsom, Jr, *New Deal or Raw Deal,* at 2 (2008).

[3] Harvard Professors Laurence Summers & Natasha Sarin, "Have Big Banks Gotten Safer?" (Brookings Papers on Economic Activity, Sept 2016) (The new regulations have harmed banks by lowering their equity values, making them "more vulnerable to adverse shocks" than before.) Summers was Director of the White House National Economic Council for Obama.

[4] Robert J. Barro, "The Job-Filled Non-Recovery" at 1, 5 (Harvard U. study, September 2016). Barro, Harvard's Warburg Professor of Economics states: "The recovery from the recent Great Recession in the U.S. (and elsewhere) has been non-existent." He points to low productivity growth and anti-market regulatory programs created by Obama as the major culprits. See also, Henry Field, *The Bumbling Colossus*, at 10-16 (amazon.com 2012).

[5] Add the 2009 $787 billion "Stimulus" – more than all previous such efforts combined – to the list of costly failures along with Dodd–Frank

and ObamaCare. Wasted on non-productive ends, the "Stimulus" utterly failed to stimulate. Neither employment nor GDP budged. Over the 8 Obama years, recovery was the slowest since WW II, GDP averaged the lowest at 2.1%, millions fell below the poverty line, national debt more than doubled, young adults began living at home into their 30's. After Obama extolled the recovery and job creation in his 2016 State of the Union speech, Bill Clinton said: "Millions and millions of people look at that pretty picture of America he painted, and they can't find themselves in it to save their lives."

[6] Jeff Jacoby, "Barack Obama's Legacy of Failure," The Boston Globe, January 8, 2017. Obama's "crossed fingers behind the back" approach regarding ObamaCare was no surprise. In the early 2000s as an Illinois state senator, Obama indicated his preference for single-payer health care like Canada, where the government runs all aspects of medicine and controls all pricing, service, and pay. In 2009-10, this proved politically impossible. As a few observers pointed out at the time, ObamaCare was actually designed to fail, drafters hoping to follow with single-payer:

> "Unable to get [total government control] outright, they created a reform bill that, while falling short, would create the conditions for a cost crisis such that complete government control becomes a seeming inevitability." (Henry Field, *The Bumbling Colossus,* at 59-60).

2

The Old Progressive Approach has Hit the Wall

2. The Old Progressive Approach Has Hit the Wall, Hard

The early Obama years featured a high water mark in the Old Progressive approach. Blessed with a filibuster-proof super-majority in the Senate and majority control in the House, the 2009-10 Democrats were able to work their will without need to listen to or compromise with the minority. And they felt the people had written them a blank check to do so. The "Stimulus", Dodd-Frank, and ObamaCare perfectly reflected this feeling.

Cracks in the wall began to appear with the bi-annual 2010 election, when Republicans captured the House. Then in 2012 the Senate flipped too, so Obama had lost the ability to impose the Old Progressive agenda via legislation. Instead, he turned to executive fiat, causing his department heads and agencies to find ways around the laws and to issue decrees regardless. Often, the courts enjoined this blatant end-run around the Constitution. Undaunted, he continued this for four years, even up to the day in 2017 the new Republican Administration was sworn in.

These last six years reflected one of the greatest shifts from one party to the other in American history. Over 1,100 elected Democrats nationwide were replaced by Republicans. Democrats lost both houses of Congress and, in 2016, the Presidency. As of 2017, Democrats held just 18 of 50 governorships, and only 31 of the nation's 99 state legislative chambers. The GOP stood stronger than any time since the 1920s.

This can only be seen as a colossal rejection of the Old Progressive approach which Obama stood for and proclaimed. As he said in 2016, "I'm not on this ballot, but everything we've done these last eight years *is* on the ballot."

Losing control over the entire federal apparatus, and most of the states, in 2016 speaks loudly to what happens when you blindly pursue the old progressive dream.

3

Time for a New Progressive Approach

3. Time for Liberals and Progressives to Adopt a New Approach

The Old Progressive approach advanced by liberals and progressives alike has hit the wall. It is an intellectual dead end. It has degenerated into executive commands telling the states how to manage transgender bathrooms. Into "resistance" by uniform "no" votes, and diffuse and symbolic protests. A disconnect exists with a large swath of the public and often, with reason and evidence. The form is still evident, but the substance is gone. It is like the old Wendy's commercial; "Where's the beef?" Time for a new approach which plants the feet firmly on the ground. Which has strong substance in a proven reality.

What would a new Progressive approach look like? First, it would adopt the ideals of the Old Progressives – to elevate the living standards of the poorest among us, provide quality education for all, and ensure everyone has truly affordable, accessible health care. A particular focus today is on the inner-city minority male, whose relative status is failing to improve.

Next, it would shed the political calculus of modern-day Democrats, which seems to elevate identity politics and interest-group commitments over ideals, which are lost amid the thunder. A new calculus should be based upon the old ideals but with real benefits to those who need them.

For example, although in recent years African-Americans have voted overwhelmingly for Democrats (over 93% for Obama), they have little to show for it. Certain African-American leaders, mainly those with powerful organizations, have benefited, but this has not trickled down to those in need. The New Progressive approach prioritizes those in need, not the embalmed leadership.

What the history set out above reveals is a stark fact; The Old Progressive approach neglects the economic understanding needed to truly advance towards the ideals held. Taking from "the rich" and redistributing to "the poor" sounds great, but harms the whole and has failed to achieve real progress. It leads to amplifying the worst kind of identity politics, where you "deserve" largess simply because of your color, ethnicity or perceived "victim" status. The shifting coterie of victims implies oppressors, implicating us all. This is politically toxic, divisive, intellectually hollow, and ultimately self-defeating.

So the first requirement of New Progressives is to come to a firm understanding of the reality of failure they have wreaked over the last decade, and start to make friends with the best economics offered. This does not mean to listen just to the few left-wing old progressives like Paul Krugman of the Princeton Economics Department and the N.Y. Times. It does not mean reading that and similar newspapers and watching TV news and thinking you are well educated and on top of things. It requires humility and a willingness to learn. It requires listening to and realizing the powerful truths in the long dominant chorus of top-notch economists who have done the work revealing the failure of what the old progressives created. Over the last fifty years these are the people who have received a string of Nobel Prizes in recognition of their achievements, work which has revolutionized economics departments and become an intellectual flood, but which has made no dent in the Old Progressive firmament.

Time for that to change. The work of these economists — briefly reviewed later — clearly describes most accurately the reality we have to deal with. The results are too powerful. Ideology which mal-describes, or continually misses the mark, as Old Progressive ideology does, should give way in favor of superior reason and evidence. An ideology which elevates your sense of morality makes you feel good, but unless it actually helps people – all the people – the whole parade is a grand illusion.

This requires a shift in the framework of thought, the unspoken but formidable social and political rules which determine what is acceptable and not acceptable to discuss, what ideas, statements, beliefs are outside the pale. For the last at least eight years, the framework has been defined largely by the rhetorical powers of the Obama Presidency, amplified by a dominant media largely enamored with it. This has both shielded and imprisoned those under its sway.

It led to the complete shock and disbelief when, on November 8, 2016, a complete political novice won over the highly experienced Obama legacy candidate, Hillary Clinton. The dominant media and liberal/progressives were uncomprehending. But the writing was clearly on the wall. They just could not see it. The reality of President Trump was baked in the lacunae: the Old Progressive belief in governance by elites, lack of respect for the common sense of the ordinary citizen, denouncing them as the cause of discriminations and poverty for others, unending expansion of welfare dependency, and ferreting out ever-smaller minorities to highlight for anti-discrimination crusades.

Somewhere in all this something big got lost. It was concern for economic growth, jobs for all those seeking or discouraged after eight long years of other priorities and for those – particularly in the inner cities – neglected and left behind.

Nothing revives the spirit and provides a moral center like a decent, productive job for someone without one. Yet from the outset, growth and jobs was most distinctly not the Obama priority. Restructuring American health care and our financial system according to old progressive templates was. Thus ensued the slowest recovery since the Great Depression, what Harvard's Warburg Professor of Economics Robert J. Barro calls an atypical, government-induced "non-recovery". And the entire Democrat Party traipsed on after like a Pied Piper.

In this way the blinders affixed by an unreal or unhelpful framework of thinking and moral reasoning lead us astray. A new party administration will affect this framework of thought. Ideas which were readily rejected as uncomfortable, obviously wrong or unworthy of consideration, will begin to emerge as part of the new discussable. Cognitive dissonance — clashing reality and thought — creates the framework, and will shift it as well.

Thus opens the door for liberals and progressives to a new approach to policy. For example, the plight of the inner-city African-American male, long trapped in generations of poverty and neglect, can begin to emerge as a discussable problem with a discussable solution. This is a large group with non-competitive development, short on proper language and work habits. It is time to deal with this. But first the thought-framework needs to shift enough so that the reality can be articulated and honestly discussed without the denial mechanism of "blaming the victim". That has not been done, nor will it be done, until the blinders of old progressivism are removed. A new freedom of speech and thought will emerge.[1]

[1] Jason L. Riley, an African American writer, notes how this thought framework limits thinking and speech about race:

"Academia also prefers to tread lightly when it comes to discussing how black culture affects racial disparities, not because social scientists believe culture plays no significant role but because saying so aloud invites charges of racism and blaming the victim. In a 2006 New York Times op-ed, Harvard sociologist Orlando Patterson [also African American] lamented 'a deep-seated dogma that has prevailed in social science and policy circles since the mid-1960s: the rejection of any explanation that invokes a group's cultural attributes—its distinctive attitudes, values and predispositions, and the resulting behavior of its members.'" 1/25/2017 WSJ.

4

The New Progressive Embraces the Market and Resists "Top-Down" Regulatory Regimes

4. "Top-Down" Regulatory Regimes Destroy the Value which the Free Market Creates

The first and most important change the New Progressive/Liberal embodies is respect for the powerful benefits of free markets. In simplest form, markets are voluntary exchanges between people, in which each sees benefit to themselves or their loved ones. Markets are "free" to the extent individuals are unconstrained by government in their choices. The benefits of freedom are psychological, emotional, spiritual — and material. Everyone is better off when able to secure and fulfill their wants as they see them. This freedom is a value to be weighed heavily in the balance, never to be neglected. Most importantly, free markets are based upon a clear morality which needs to be understood. As we shall see, through the alchemy of free markets, the individual value of freedom and the pursuit of self interest transmutes into benefit for the whole in a way no scheme of government controls can.

Like other old progressives, Obama professed to be a fan of free markets. But his actions spoke otherwise. When push came to shove, the impulse to reach for the regulatory club inevitably prevailed. And this was not just little things, here and there around the edges. It was to bring huge areas of the American economy – health care and finance – under government control.[1]

The result is a disaster. ObamaCare failed to live up to most of its promises, costs zoomed, and coverage, where enabled, shrank. Most new enrollees have to contend with the thin soup of Medicaid. Dodd-Frank has wreaked less visible harms, but they are just as profound. Costs of compliance keep smaller banks down, and the ganglia of rules and uncertainty slowed job creation and discouraged millions of workers from staying in the work force. To top it off, we are no safer from bank failures, according to Larry Summers, one of President Obama's chief economic advisers, who helped shape these regulations. [2]

Not only did people lose freedom, they suffer increasing costs, significantly worse choices and a less bright future.

These regulatory regimes were no light toss-offs. They were crafted by the "best and the brightest". They followed the dictates of old progressivism – experts at the helm, disregard for the savvy and common sense of ordinary people, prolix, confusing, sweeping displacement of business judgment and markets, and substitution of experienced, hands-on buyers and sellers with remote bureaucrats, issuing rules.

Each of these was exactly the opposite of what is needed. That these carefully crafted enactments have failed so spectacularly, as many predicted they would, should cause thinking people to realize that something is amiss in the assumptions underlying the old progressive/liberal approach. Always claiming the moral high ground, championing chosen victims, demanding public action may be self-satisfying, but has proven foolhardy. A harmful illusion. Perhaps now a dawning respect grows for what was displaced and scorned – the free market's demonstrable power for good.[3]

The Illusion that Regulation Improves Markets

Along with that realization comes education on our own experiences with the "cure" of industry regulation and how it has failed its promises and cost our people. This is an education liberal and old progressive health care experts have studiously neglected to face. Starting with the

New Deal in the 1930s, we have experience with numerous regulatory regimes and much has been learned by careful later analysis of how they turned out. The bottom line is not happy for those wedded to the idea of industry regulation and control as cure-all for the perceived ills of economic life.[4]

Perhaps the best summary is by the great Nobel-Prize winning economist Ronald Coase, whose career was largely spent working out the economic effects of regulated industries:

> "I have referred to studies of the regulation of natural gas and drugs. But there have also been studies of the regulation of many diverse activities such as agriculture, aviation, banking, broadcasting, electricity supply, milk distribution, railroads and trucking, taxicabs, whiskey labeling, and zoning. I mention only studies with which I am familiar; there are doubtless many others. The main lesson to be drawn from these studies is clear: They all tend to suggest that the regulation is either ineffective or that, when it has a noticeable impact, on balance the effect is bad, so that consumers obtain a worse product or a higher-priced product or both as a result of the regulation. Indeed, this result is found so uniformly as to create a puzzle: One would expect to find, in all these studies, at least some government programs that do more good than harm."[5]

This is not to say that all regulation is bad: indeed, as Coase emphasized, some regulation or rules are needed for free markets to function well. Strong laws protecting property rights and proscribing undue influence, fraud and abuse. Independent courts to enforce them. And some rules lower transaction costs and promote trust. The simple example of a stock exchange is revealing. Long before the state ever thought to regulate stock buying and selling, informal rules were developed by the participants to help them effect transactions, rules as to type, number, time, security, and the like.

So what decides if one kind of regulation is better or worse? It is the *intrusive* regulatory regimes which do the most harm, government telling the industry actors how to exercise their business judgment. Prime example: HUD and the 2007-8 financial crash, discussed later. The worst regulations profess great benefits which are minor or illusory in fact but actually impose costly hidden burdens deterring competition, reducing innovation, raising costs or prices, and making it harder for people to transact. Examples: Dodd-Frank, ObamaCare, certain interest-group driven zoning and building code restrictions. Helpful rules promote transactions, foster competition, allow free pricing to reflect true scarcities and preferences, and foster the free flow of commerce. Examples: anti-fraud laws, anti-discrimination laws, Sherman Anti-Trust, ordinary traffic laws.

Textbooks Promoting Myths

The old liberal/progressive mind-set favoring government intervention in markets has become firmly fixed in many people who have imbibed the message from home or school. Tragically, for decades many of our most distinguished historians, versed in their own type of research but uneducated in economics, have produced college and secondary texts painting an erroneous view of markets as harmful and government as savior (e.g., Arthur Schlesinger, Jr, David Kennedy, C. Vann Woodward, Henry Steele Commager). Ask almost any liberal or progressive what they think of the New Deal or 19th century industrialists, and you get an answer echoing this view. Robber Barons. Chaos reigning in markets, creating harm. Rapacious, greedy, business needing to be tamed by government control.

Modern, economically sound research has turned this view on its head, but few old progressives bother to, or can, listen. Cognitive dissonance — the clash of ideas and reality — plugs the ears and stops the brain. Onward their thought-framework chugs like a train careening off the tracks.[6]

[1] The "top-down" mind-set also led to heavy-handed, misguided efforts in education, detailed in Frederick M. Hess, "The Real Obama Education Record," 25 *National Affairs* at 3-19 (Fall 2015)(wasting

early bi-partisan support, his "education-reform agenda amounted to a stimulus-funded race to bureaucracy"); see also Field, *The Bumbling Colossus* at 50-60, 201-208 (amazon.com 2012).

[2] See Ch. 1, footnotes 3-7 above. Description "helped shape" is from Summers' website.

[3] Chapter 8 particularly discusses the powerful benefits and poorly understood morality of free markets. For further definition of free markets and discussion of the issues and benefits, see Field, *The Bumbling Colossus* at 147-190 (amazon.com 2012), and www.thebumblingcolossus.com.

[4] Discussed in chapters 5, 9, and later. A good source is *Chicago Studies in Political Economy*, ed. by Nobel laureate George J. Stigler, at 209-537 (U. Chicago Press 1988). Those seeking a fuller discussion of these issues should read Field, *The Bumbling Colossus*, Ch. VII "Experiences with Regulation; How it Ends up Protecting Select Private Interests at the Expense of the Public" (amazon.com 2012), and the website www.thebumblingcolossus.com.

[5] Ronald H. Coase, "Economists and Public Policy", in *Essays on Economics and Economists*, at 61 (U. of Chicago Press 1994). Another example is the FDA, popularly believed of unequivocal benefit. But the harms may outweigh the benefits. Yasuta, "Food Safety Regulation in the United States", 15 *The Independent Review,* at 209, 221. (Fall 2010)("Government intervention, claimed to correct market inefficiency, creates another situation of inefficiency."). A convincing case for reform.

Persons in favor of civil rights for all should favor free markets, since contrary to the common view that capitalists profit from discrimination, in truth the return to capital suffers in competitive industries if discrimination goes on. Labor however may benefit; hence union resistance. Gary S. Becker, *The Economics of Discrimination,* at 13 (U. Chicago Press 1957)(received 1992 Nobel Prize in Economics).

[6] Professor Burton W. Folsom, Jr. illuminatingly discusses these historians' textbooks in detail at Chapter 7 of Folsom, *The Myth of the Robber Barons* (6th ed, 2010)("If we seriously study entrepreneurs, the state, and the rise of big business in the United States we will have to sacrifice the textbook morality play of "greedy businessmen" fleecing the public until at last they are stopped by the actions of the state."). Also, Folsom, *New Deal or Raw Deal*, chapter 17 "Why Historians Have Missed the Mark" (Simon & Schuster 2008)("In the progressive view [including historians], intentions and sincerity are among the noblest virtues ... compassion, not results, is the best answer."). But the millions suffering unemployment during the New Deal's long non-recovery probably cared more about results than compassionate intentions. Ditto during the Obama years. Real benefit trumps empathy and good intentions every time, regardless of common misconceptions.

5

Single-Payer Systems Attract, but Destroy

5. The Single-Payer Siren Song Lures, But Wrecks the Boat

If extensive government regulation through bureaucracies is not a helpful way to improve our health care, it follows *mutatis mutandis* that total government control will prove even worse. And indeed this is the case in every country in which government control has been effected. Like the Sirens of Greek myth, advocates of single payer health sing a sweet song which attracts the unwary unto the rocks. If you want ever-increasing waiting lists, spiraling costs to the treasury, decline in investment, ever-decreasing quality of service, and nothing like the equality promised, single-payer or socialized medicine is for you.

Start with Canada, the country most often touted as a possible model for America. Sally C. Pipes, having spent her career either living in Canada's single-payer system or studying its effects, summarizes as follows:

> "Today, after thirty years of government intervention, the system suffers from:
>
> - Long waiting times for critical procedures
> - Lack of access to current technology
> - Increasing costs to taxpayers and patients, and
> - A brain drain of doctors".[1]

Similarly, other top-notch experts examining numerous countries across the globe which adopted government controlled health care have found the gap between promise and performance starkly revealing:

- "Wherever national health insurance has been tried, rationing by waiting is pervasive – with waits that force patients to endure pain and sometimes put their lives at risk
- Not only is health care not equal, if anything it tends to correlate with income – with the middle class getting more access than the poor, and the rich getting more access than the middle class, especially when income class is weighted by incidence of illness
- Not only are health care resources not allocated on the basis of need, those systems tend to overspend on the relatively healthy while denying the truly sick access to specialist care and life-saving medical technology
- And far from establishing national priorities that get care first to those who need it most, these systems leave rationing choices up to local bureaucracies that, for example, fill hospital beds with chronic patients while acute patients wait for care." [2]

The harms inflicted by socialized or single-payer systems occur because they violate the most fundamental economic principles:

> "Countries with single-payer health insurance limit health care spending by limiting supply. … The consequence of making health care free, thus creating unconstrained demand, while limiting supply, is that demand exceeds supply for virtually every service. That, in turn, leads to rationing, usually by forcing patients to wait for treatment." (Goodman, Musgrave, & Herrick, *Lives at Risk; Single-Payer National Health Insurance Around the World,* at 18)

> "These numbers are getting worse over time, not better. By 2008, over one million Britons were waiting for hospital care. Another 200,000 were *waiting to get on a waiting list.* Canada, with only 33 million people, had 800,000 on wait lists. Fifteen years ago, in Canada the average wait between referral by primary care physician to specialist was nine weeks; by 2008, it was fifteen weeks." Field, *The Bumbling Colossus,* at 100, with data from Sally C. Pipes, *The Top Ten Myths of American Health Care,* at 125.

Although the dream of free, universal care run by government dies hard, die it should. A meretricious road to harm, particularly alluring to the well-intended idealist. But seeing this requires removing one's blinders imposed by old progressive ideology and its repetition from political and media sources caring more about catering to their own followers than about evidence and reality.

The Unavoidable Dilemma of Public Control

The dilemma inherent in single-payer and other forms of government controlled health care is as follows: if you increase access and levels of service, you greatly enlarge costs. If you try to contain costs, you inevitably cut service and/or its availability. This vicious trade-off is hidden from the public. Costs are lost in general budgets, so people are misled to believe all is well. Accountability is non-existent.

In England, this finally came a cropper. After WW II, England created its British National Health Service, which controlled all aspects of the people's health care. For a long time, it was a high point of national pride and promoted as a beacon for the world. Free and universal. But after 60 years or so, its foundations were found to be cracked and broken. A government study in 2010 found that "the NHS simply cannot continue to afford to support the costs of the existing bureaucracy" because "the reality is that there is no more money." The study frankly admits that the "top-down" socialist model upon which the NHS was based led to bureaucratic bloat, neglect of patient needs, and decline of service and quality. Instead, it advises a "revolution" in approach, where "the money follows the patient", what it calls "patient power".[3]

Only market-based systems avoid the dilemma of trading off access and costs. Markets allow people to seek the greatest value — best service or product at lowest cost. Providers are incentivized to compete with improved offerings and reduced prices. We have the example of Singapore (discussed in the next chapter), which thirty-five years ago rejected the British government-controlled NHS model and has had marked success with market-based health care based, as here, on individual or family medical accounts.

[1] Sally C. Pipes, *Miracle Cure: How to Solve America's Health Care Crisis and Why Canada Isn't the Answer*, at 150 (Pacific Research Institute and the Fraser Institute 2004).

[2] Goodman, Musgrave & Herrick, *Lives at Risk: Single-Payer National Health Insurance Around the World* at 9, 12 (Roman & Littlefield 2004)("The failure of national health insurance is a secret of modern social science. ...scholars failed to understand the defects..." and "advocates and ordinary citizens hold an idealized view of it.") For further discussion including analysis of the claims of single-payer proponents, see Field, *The Bumbling Colossus*, at 88-118, "The Single-Payer Mirage".

[3] *Equity and Excellence: Liberating the NHS*, a "White Paper" submitted by the Prime Minister and others to Parliament, July 2010 (available on the internet). Singapore's refusal to adopt Britain's "top-down" socialized NHS and success with a market-based approach based on individual medical accounts is a clear object lesson in how to avoid the invidious trade-off intrinsic to single-payer and other state-controlled systems where greater access magnifies costs and cutting costs diminishes quality. Read William A. Haseltine, "Affordable Excellence: The Singapore Healthcare Story" (Brookings Institution Press 2013).

6

Moving Beyond the Old Progressive Thought-Framework Box

6. Where Conservative and Progressive Meet: the HSA Solution

So if government controlled systems are dead ends, how do we start to think about creating a health care system for this country which meets our goals – universal coverage, truly affordable, without skyrocketing costs or burdens on the public and the taxpayer? In other words, something that fulfills the old progressive ideals but without the rigor mortis of top-down bureaucratic death and decline. The English 2010 White Paper offers a clue: Patient Power. How can we empower the patient without the bureaucracy, the huge costs, and the dependency which the top-down approach creates?

The answer, it turns out, is right in front of our faces. For many years, Congress has approved people employing special accounts dedicated to the health needs of themselves and their families, into which monies can be placed which are tax deductible going in, grow tax-free, and are tax-free when spent. The only restriction is that the sums be spent just for health care, and that the account be linked to high deductible health insurance covering all substantial ("catastrophic") health needs. These accounts are called "Health Savings Accounts" (HSAs).

So with HSAs you are covered for all substantial, catastrophic health risks under the linked policy, and for routine things under the deductible you pay directly out of the HSA with tax-free money. The premium is far less, since routine costs are excluded from coverage and you can tailor coverage to your needs. Costs beneath the high deductible are paid from tax-free money you have contributed into the account. Everyone should be required to have these to participate in the benefits, like a social security account. Contribution limits and other rules presently encumbering these accounts need to be changed.

What about people unable to afford the premium or the costs beneath the deductible? Here's where government plays a funding role. To achieve universality, government pays into their HSA accounts, by credits or vouchers, enough to provide for this. What about existing federal health subsidy programs like Medicare, Medicaid, CHIP? Ensure every person eligible has an HSA. This way no one loses coverage. How to fund them? Much of the money which currently government pays directly to providers – hospitals, doctors, service groups, etc. – is paid instead to the patient, who is thereby enabled to spend his own money to effect his own choices. Choice of provider, doctor, hospital, testing service, insurance carrier, the whole banana. A neat solution.

Notice what this simple change does. By empowering the patient with the power of the purse, everyone in the health care universe looks to the patient, not the doctor, the bureaucrat, the politician. The basis for a competitive world is reestablished, people competing for the patient's dollar. A market for health services revives.

In this way we meld the ideals of old progressivism with the economic approach required to make them relevant and helpful in today's world. The practical benefits of markets are supported and enhanced. They are brought to everyone's front door. Everyone has health care, routine and catastrophic, when they need it. As for costs? One of the greatest benefits of markets is that competition drives lower costs while also ensuring that quality of service or product is maintained. If your service or product is seen as lesser, or more expensive than a similar one, the patient goes elsewhere. People can choose a lower quality plan for a lower cost, or a higher quality plan for a higher cost. But the system based upon free markets and competition ensures that they have this choice. Overall, costs will tend downward rather than up as marginal efforts reduce prices, just like they do in all competitive markets across the globe.

Advocates of government controlled systems do not like HSAs. ObamaCare for example restricts their use by severely limiting the amounts which can be contributed. The reason for this is that they want to force everyone into their giant, mandated pools with uniform coverage and ever higher costs.

But these giant mandated pools are a disaster. Costs skyrocket. Revolt from them along with the rest of ObamaCare was largely why the Democrats have lost politically since 2010.

The case for building a new system around HSAs rests on the assumption that Americans of all economic level, social stripe, ethnic derivation, race, sex and the rest are capable of, and largely desirous of, having some control over their own health care choices. This assumption of independence is the opposite of ObamaCare, which assumed people are incompetent to make these choices and prefer someone else (misnamed "experts" in universities and think tanks or bureaucracies fumbling in the dark) to make them instead. And when you concede this responsibility, you also concede power over your own purse – the costs of all health items. Taxes and premiums escalate and you have no power to alter them. A Devil's bargain.

We should also move away from all-inclusive, soup-to-nuts group insurance such as offered through employment. With low or no-deductibles, the premiums are horrible and getting worse, since everything and everyone is included, routine or not. This violates the first rule of insurance, which is that it is to cover risks, not certainties. Routine visits, tests, etc. are not risks, they are certainties, and this type of health care expense should not be part of insurance. Instead, we should move to higher-deductible insurance covering real risks, substantial threats and costs. This is precisely what is required with HSAs. Their universal availability will encourage this shift.

The same reasoning applies to preexisting conditions. These are no longer risks, but are by definition known and certain. Therefore, they should not be part of a general insurance system. Instead, they should be carved off into separate, publicly supported funds or exchanges.[1]

Singapore's Lesson in Free Market Empowerment

Will it work? We have a real life example in what Singapore has done over the last 35 years with its health care. They created a universal market-based system close to what is set out here. In a detailed analysis titled "Affordable Excellence; The Singapore Healthcare Story" (Brookings Institution Press 2013), William A. Haseltine, noted Professor at Harvard Medical School, biochemical researcher and biotech entrepreneur, describes their accomplishment. Singapore, a country of over five million, requires all workers and employers to contribute to "MediSave" individual and family medical savings accounts. These and related accounts are "the cornerstone" of their system. Realizing the negatives with single-payer and other state-controlled approaches, in 1993 a Ministerial "White Paper" set out goals, since followed. These were to "promote individual responsibility for one's own health and avoid over-reliance on state welfare or third-party medical insurance", and "engage competition and market forces to improve service and raise efficiency." All-inclusive "first-dollar" coverage with low or no deductibles like our group employee plans were discouraged in favor of high deductible coverage. "Free" care was seen as a false path — "contributing to a welfare state mentality."

The result? "Singapore has achieved extraordinary results both in high quality of its healthcare system and in controlling the cost of care." Sixth in the world in health outcomes while spending less on healthcare than any other high-income country, on both a per capita and percentage of GDP basis. Their universal HSA-type system is effective in "keeping costs low without sacrificing quality". No single-payer of other government-controlled system can come close to this achievement at many times the cost.

Responsibility for this rests clearly upon its adoption of a market-based approach centering on individual and family medical accounts. State-controlled systems can not avoid the invidious trade-off where

increasing quality raises costs, and controlling costs reduces quality.
Only a market-based approach can raise quality while reducing costs.

[1] The plan set out here — universal HSAs/vouchers/split-off of pre-
existing conditions into a public fund — tracks closely the approach
of Nobel Prize-winning economist Gary S. Becker. See Becker and
Becker, *The Economics of Life*, at 40-42 (McGraw-Hill 1997)("The
federal role should be to ensure that all families are protected against
major illness."). He estimates that making this plan universal, including
replacing Medicare & Medicaid, would cost about the same as presently
we pay for those two programs alone.

The best recent estimate of the cost of the exchanges for preexisting
conditions, apart from Medicaid, is about $16 -20 billion, less than a
third the cost of ObamaCare's $56 billion in subsidies for 2016. Betsy
McCaughey, "How Many ObamaCare Patients Have Pre-Existing
Conditions?", 1/18/2017 *WSJ*.

7

What are the Basics of a Universal HSA System?

7. The Simplicity and Satisfaction of a Universal HSA System

The following basic elements will achieve the goals set out as progressive ideals become concrete realities, and a universal, cost-constrained, high service health care for all is achieved. Cover Everyone and Put the Patient in Charge.

1. Universality: everyone should have either an individual or family Health Savings Account, recast for this purpose. This automatically means they have a high-deductible insurance plan covering all substantial health costs — so-called "catastrophic" coverage. All routine or smaller costs below the deductible are paid from the tax-free money which has been accumulating in the HSA. Money placed in the HSA is tax-deductible, and growth in investments is tax-free. The tax-free feature is also needed to equalize between this and employment-based group coverage, for which the provision of insurance is not deemed "income" to the employee. This anomaly has provided an incentive to sweep everything into these plans, greatly exaggerating costs.

2. Public Support for the Poor: those unable to fund their HSAs receive adequate funding from state or federal sources, by credits or vouchers placed in their HSA and redeemable only at legitimate doctors or hospitals. This enables them to choose and pay for the insurance coverage which best suits their needs, and also fund the routine costs and expenses below the deductible.

The amount of support is aligned with income and generously scaled to encourage saving, perhaps with matching grants above the poverty line, and so as not to create an inadvertent "tax" on escaping poverty.

3. Preexisting Conditions: Insurance is to guard against adverse risks, not certainties. Yet preexisting conditions are known and certain. Therefore, they should not be part of normal insurance. Nor should routine visits. Yet our group insurance supplied by employers, and public programs following their lead like Medicare and Medicaid have done so. This grossly inflates costs for all and undermines the financial integrity of the system. Worse, ObamaCare includes a mandate that all preexisting conditions be covered in all policies.

Instead, the social/political choice to cover preexisting conditions is best met by separating them out for special public-support. Doing this recognizes this coverage is a public policy, not a market feature, and allows insurers to bid for the business in the existing state-based exchanges, with policies funded by state or federal sources. This allows the market for true insurance to better function without distortion. Persons with preexisting conditions will therefore be covered as to their true risks through their HSAs and the preexisting conditions will be carved off to the exchanges.

4. Eliminate Most Required Mandates & Controls on What is Covered: Key drivers of escalating costs are the 2000+ mandates and controls on coverage imposed by the states and, since ObamaCare, by the federal government. Such matters as naturopaths, morbid obesity treatment, wigs, chiropractors, podiatrists, massage therapists, drug abuse treatment, mental health and the like should not be mandated for everyone. If someone wants the coverage they are free to get and pay for it. Insurers will respond where demand exists. Forcing everyone to pay for coverage they neither want nor perhaps believe in is unfair, hugely costly, and should be stopped.

5. Allow Interstate Sales of Health Insurance: There is no reason to continue the current prohibition on interstate sales. States will continue to supervise and monitor the safely and solvency of insurers domiciled in the state, as is now the case. Allowing this aids competition among insurers, which lowers costs and increases patient choice.

6. Promote Information on Prices and Costs: Today, few medical practices and hospitals can readily price their services other than by following the Medicare-inspired breakdowns universally adhered to. Patients need to have true information on what medical services will cost. This informs their choices. In time, private services will fill the gap, but government may need to encourage such initially as the change in expectations adapts to the new circumstances of competition and patient choice.

7. Convert Medicare, Medicaid and CHIP to an HSA Approach: There is no substantial reason why age or economic level should restrict people from participating in "patient power" markets. Over time, these huge public programs should be integrated into the HSA system. Do this soon so no one loses coverage.

There should also be a fund for super-costly multiple catastrophes which exceed coverage limits. This can be privately funded with public backup. Available only if certain high limits are in the HSA coverage. This will prevent bankruptcy due to the unforeseen.

Two related issues are the high cost of drugs and medical liability insurance. On drugs, the FDA's overly stringent process can be readily streamlined, focusing less on efficacy and mostly on safety, potentially cutting development costs by half. Liability insurance is driven largely by state law of pain & suffering damages, an open invitation for jury excess. Limiting them to say, 3x actual damages would solve this. Beware the political power of the tort bar, which has log-jammed state jury award reform efforts in the past.

The transition from the present to an HSA-based universal system can be effected by legislation providing everyone with an HSA, and funding for the poor. Persons with group employment-based coverage will have a period to choose. Older Medicare recipients can choose to remain. Medicaid recipients get an HSA and funding, with time to acclimate.

We All Benefit When the Conservative and Progressive Have Merged

With patients controlling their own purse strings, prices will come down and service will be maintained, as normal competitive forces reengage in today's moribund health world. The result will be the opposite of what we see around the world in government controlled health systems, where, absent a market, the unholy trade-off exists so that every effort to constrain costs inevitably harms service, creating ever-longer wait lists, restricting access to new technology, limiting investment, and driving doctors and other service providers off-shore.

8

Virtue and Well-Being in the Free Markets

8. The Special Morality, Virtue and Well-Being of Free Markets

The beauty of a "bottom-up" system where the patient has the power of the purse and real choice is that providers are focused not on satisfying the wants and desires of doctors and hospitals, or politicians, but those of the patient. Competition for his or her business inevitably means that somewhat magically and spontaneously costs are constrained and service is maintained or enhanced, not the reverse. We will learn again the power of Adam Smith's Paradox, where regardless of an individual person's motives of self-gain, the greater society is served. Speaking of the ordinary business person, Smith noted that since each individual directs his industry where

> "its produce may be of the greatest value, [so] every individual necessarily labours to render the annual revenue of society as great as he can. He generally, indeed, neither intends to promote the public interest, nor knows how much he is promoting it....; and by directing that industry in such a manner as its product may be of the greatest value, he intends only his own gain, and he is in this, as in many other cases, led by an invisible hand to promote an end which was no part of his intention. Nor is it worse for the society that it was no part of it. By promoting his own interest he frequently promotes that of the society more effectually than when he actually intends to promote it."[1]

Many people confuse the self interest Smith describes with egocentric "all for me" attitudes. First, this neglects Smith's Paradox, which describes how people intending only their own advantage in a business transaction nonetheless benefit the whole. In addition, participation in markets forces a discipline upon those transacting, for no one wants to deal with a cheater, or a fraud, or a tout of inferior goods, or someone seeking to charge more than the market price. A reputation for honesty, reliability and diligence is a key to market success. Thus a discipline ensuring morality and virtue is built into the core of the market system.

Two Worlds: Market Morality and the Limits of Benevolence

Many would prefer if people acted from benevolence and to benefit others rather than from what Smith called "self-love" and what we call self-interest. It is common among liberals and progressives to state, for example, that conservatives, or people who advocate the "free market", lack heart or compassion. They believe that compassion and good intentions override all considerations of economics when discussing the welfare of individuals or groups. They apply to the economy, including the market, the same benevolent morality they apply in their family, small affinity group, or church. So they decry reliance on or promotion of "the free market" as cold and heartless, preferring endless government interventions based upon benevolence.

But this thinking misses a key reality. Free markets deliver unique benefits and have lifted mankind out of poverty over the last two hundred years as no government program ever could have, and free markets cannot survive on benevolence. Certainly benevolence is often a motive, especially within families. But benevolence wanes the farther away and more remote the object. Regrettable though this may be, it is a real and natural limitation. Smith famously used the example of the fabrication of a pin, and a woolen coat, whose multiple sources are supremely remote and complex. As Ronald Coase explains:

> "To rely on benevolence to bring about an adequate division of labor is an impossibility. We need the cooperation of multitudes, many of whom we do not know and for whom we can therefore feel no benevolence nor can they feel such for us. ... Adam

Smith's main point, as I see it, is not that benevolence or love is *not* the basis of economic life in a modern society, but that it *cannot be*. We have to rely on the market, with its motive force, self-interest. If man were so constituted that he only responded to feelings of benevolence, we would still be living in caves with lives "nasty, brutish and short". The efficient working of the market thus becomes the key to the maintenance of a comfortable standard of living and to its increase." ("The Wealth of Nations" in *Essays on Economics and Economists*, at 81-82 (U. Chicago Press 1994).

The free market — what F. A. Hayek calls "the extended order of human cooperation" (*The Fatal Conceit; The Errors of Socialism*, U. Chicago, at 6-28 (1988)) — has to operate on a different morality than the beneficent personal morality found among family, church groups or small tribes, which is based on self-sacrifice, empathy, compassion, community, "all for one, one for all". Free markets operate on cooperation, trust, reliability, honesty, discipline, but not on self-sacrifice or benevolence. This is not a preference or option, it is an unavoidable fact.

Therein lies the rub. The enormous increase in prosperity and freedom over the last two hundred years could not have occurred if benevolence replaced self-interest. Why is this? It is because modern economies depend on free pricing. Prices convey the information needed on the real wants and preferences of the innumerable individuals both up and down the supply/demand chain, and all potential alternatives, which constantly change, and only if they act on their self-interest does the price reflect what they really want. Benevolence destroys the truth and value of the information, and this destroys the market and its benefits. In economic-talk, resources are misallocated, and the total social product is diminished. Everyone is short-changed.

The impersonal morality of markets and the compassionate morality of family/tribe often overlap (nothing excludes people in markets from acting benevolently if they want), but they are not interchangeable. In most cases, the market supplies the want better than benevolence would. Help to raise your friend's barn if it burns, but note that next time he should simply obtain insurance.

The fact is, all efforts to apply compassionate personal family or tribe morality to extended markets end up destroying them, putting us back (as Coase puts it) "in caves", with all that means in loss of freedoms. Similarly, applying market morality to families or tribes — by eliminating benevolence and acting only with self-interest — destroys the fabric which binds them. Families and tribes can't exist on self-interest any more than markets can on benevolence or love.

As Hayek points out, we must learn to live in two worlds at once, with their different essential moralities — the communal world of the family and tribe, with its attractions of solidarity and closeness, and the broader world of the market — the extended order of human cooperation which brings the advances, demands, stresses, and freedoms we know. It is not easy to balance these two worlds, and "our instincts often threaten to topple the whole edifice." This conflict is "the major theme of the history of civilization;"

> "It seems that Columbus recognized at once that the life of the 'savages' he encountered was more gratifying to innate human instincts. ... I believe that an atavistic longing for the life of the noble savage is the main source of the collectivist tradition."

Regrettably, few tribes of "noble savages" exist today and almost all humans are dependent upon civilization and markets. This has long been so. Anthropologists have unearthed items in ancient digs which could only have come from half way around the world. The migratory Sami of Finnmark live in tents but depend on trade with remote cultures and have for thousands of years. So seeking that gratifying past is an exercise in nostalgia, and unattainable without doing great violence — profoundly destroying the livelihood, culture and ways which the modern world has developed and upon which most all of us depend. No surprise that every effort to impose communal systems has proved impossible without great violence to those unfortunate enough to be subject to them.

The irony of living in these "two worlds" at once was summed up by Adam Smith, who pointed out that each of us "stands at all times in need of the cooperation and assistance of great multitudes, while his whole life is scarce sufficient to gain the friendship of a few persons."

This is an inescapable reality, and failure to understand it leads many well-meaning people into profound intellectual error and to promoting great harms. Free markets, and their companions, individual rights orientation and freedom in commerce (so-called "capitalism"), become the target of opprobrium and scorn. We see this every day. Much of the hostility of radical Islamists to "the West", and pulpit religion to commerce, flows from this error. So too, does the hostility of the followers of Karl Marx and other socialists to private property and commerce. From this error also flows the present-day hostility of old progressives, builders of the Regulatory State, to free markets, revealed daily in their flagship organ, the New York Times. More recently, devotees of "critical theory" or "social justice" gin up elaborate intellectual edifices propounding power and structural theories, and seeking to apply benevolence, the goal and effect of which is to destroy the free market and its individual freedom/rights basis.

Perhaps well intended, but each of these intellectual constructs is ignorant of the distinct moral basis of markets and is dangerous to all who fall victim to them. This is not some novel insight. Adam Smith saw this danger two hundred and fifty years ago. F.A. Hayek wrote *The Road to Serfdom* (1944) explicitly explaining it to a world largely under the spell of anti-market beliefs, and all the significant work in economics since only confirms the need to avoid falling prey to them. The well-meaning intellectual is especially susceptible, seduced by schemes to impose the supposed "public interest" on markets by regulation, public ownership, and similar false roads. Almost always, this urge is based, at bottom, on the misapplication of family or small group morality to markets.

The Dark Side of Empathy and Community; "We" vs "Them"

So it is that well-meaning people seeking the expansion of "community" and the universe of benevolence to markets are met with what Dwight Lee calls "the dark side of emotional morality." The more a society or group is bound together by common feeling, the greater the chance of hostility towards outsiders. Inevitably, objectives differ among groups, generating animosity and conflict. "We" vs. "Them". History and current events are rife with this. Recent examples range from the eugenically inspired "final solution" and mass murders of WW II, to today's radical Islamic terrorism, to benighted "critical theory"/"social justice" followers on campuses shutting down those simply seeking their freedom of thought and speech in a place devoted to protecting it.

Even the increasingly hostile division of Democrats and Republicans, progressives and liberals vs conservatives, shows this, albeit in muted form.

"Tribal" or group hostility to the "other" — those who are "not us" — is ubiquitous in life. But commerce works differently. A sign maker, of whatever political stripe, is probably indifferent whether an order for 100,000 signs for a political campaign comes from a Republican or Democrat. In that way, the "extended order of human cooperation" which is global commerce, with all its imperfections, is a force for civility and peace. As J. R. Clark and Dwight R. Lee put it:

> "Unfortunately, when our differences are politicized there is a real risk that the celebration will involve some high octane fireworks, as illustrated by recent events in the Middle East and other global hot spots. The setting most conducive to social harmony is one in which we can each pursue our own objectives in ways that help others pursue theirs, no matter how different these objectives may be. This is exactly what the impersonal exchanges of the marketplace facilitate, which explains why markets do far more to promote harmony among diverse people than attempts to reach agreement on common objectives."   .....

> "No one would argue that commercial pursuits can motivate us

all to join hands and sing "We Are the World". But the mundane [impersonal] morality of commerce and trade does not have to do a great job promoting social harmony to outperform the magnanimous [tribal] morality we inherited from our hunter-gatherer ancestors."

Why Government Intervention Intended to Help, Harms

Nor can the hard truth of the above be avoided by substituting the supposed benevolence of government. We have seen that government ownership or intrusive regulation of business creates more harm than good. Other, less noted, examples abound. Take the constant popular urge to fix prices of drugs or other high value items, such as the periodic calls to "freeze" the price of gas and oil, or prevent "price-gouging" during shortages. Again, we can hardly improve today on what Adam Smith pointed out, using the example of corn, almost 250 years ago:

> "When the government, in order to remedy the inconvenience of a dearth, orders all the dealers to sell their corn at what it supposes a reasonable price, it either hinders them from bringing it to market, which may sometimes produce a famine even in the beginning of the season, or if they bring it thither, it enables the people, and thereby encourages them to consume it so fast, as must necessarily produce a famine before the end of the season. The unlimited, unrestrained freedom of the corn trade, as it is the only effectual preventative of the miseries of a famine, so it is the best palliative of the inconveniences of a dearth."

As Coase notes, "Could we do much better today if we were discussing government control of the price of oil and natural gas?"

Mess with free pricing and you destroy the information needed for supply to meet demand. You destroy the information needed for income and wealth creation. Stifle the profit motive and you stifle innovation, a key driver of economic progress. This reality is the shoals upon which socialized and regulated systems founder.

Disregarding this, the Soviet Union and its central price setting agency Goskomsten lost the information of true prices and debased the economy over time, which stagnated and finally imploded from within. The same happens with regulated industries (remember the decline of the railroads under the ICC), although the stagnation and decline occurs less visibly to the busy eye. Decline, waste, and stagnation are universal attributes of intrusive government intervention into free markets. Would today's vibrant world of communication technology have been conceivable were the government still sheltering AT&T with a legal regulated monopoly?

Intrusive government regulation introduces additional harms by creating privileges and favoritisms benefiting a few at the expense of the many. Adam Smith saw this. His opposition to extensive government action

> "did not arise simply because he thought it was unnecessary, but because he felt that government action would usually make matters worse. He thought governments lacked both the knowledge and the motivation to do a satisfactory job in regulating an economic system. This is because government regulations will normally be much influenced by those who stand to benefit from them, with the result that they are not necessarily advantageous to society." (Coase, ibid.)

Today we call this "regulatory capture" and the reality is well established, for which we can thank the careful studies of, among others, George J. Stigler and his "The Theory of Economic Regulation" (*Chicago Studies in Political Economy,* at 209 (1971)(Nobel Prize in Economics 1982). "Public Choice" studies (for which James M. Buchanan received the Nobel Prize in 1986) – showing how much of the behavior of "public service" or "public interest" bureaucrats and politicians is explained by their self-interest — elaborate this. The theory of "rents" or excess rewards from taking advantage of political enactments, explained by Gordon Tullock and others, shows how public regulation of industry transmutes benign well-meaning social motives into embedded select private advantages and public harms. (discussed in chapters 13-14)

All in all, it is hard to contest Smith's observation, so demonstrated in the times since, that "Great nations are never impoverished by private, though they sometimes are by public prodigality and misconduct." Every socialist scheme that has been tried has failed to improve the lot of ordinary people — bringing instead decline and disappointment. Examples: Venezuela, Cuba, Soviet Russia and satellites, North Korea, Mao's China, every nationalized industry, single-payer efforts. Failures too are our recent experiments with intrusive government control of markets in Dodd-Frank and ObamaCare. As the song goes, "When will we ever learn?"

We have far more to fear from government trying to "improve" on markets than we do from private efforts to take advantage of us. One reason for this is that government interventions are long-lasting and become imbedded. They create winners who are few and who benefit hugely, and can efficiently exercise political influence to create and maintain their privilege. The losers, consumers and potential competitors, are many and widely dispersed, and lack the means or incentive to resist.

Neglecting this, many people uneducated in the deeper moral meaning of Adam Smith's paradox and the free market pursue false paths seeking an imagined improvement in affairs through government, such as socialism, populism, old progressives, extensive and intrusive regulation, "critical theory", welfare statism, nationalism, "social justice", single-payer health, and other detours. Most often, these blind alleys derive from misguided attempts to apply family/church beneficence to the extended market. Instead of imagined benefits, they end up destroying the free market's moral order and its "hand that feeds". The imagined benefits prove elusive and non-existent, the harms devastating.

End Notes; Doing Good with Self-Interest

This leads to an irony. Charity is, and always has been, an integral part of free markets, especially benefited by the additions created over basic need. But although charity rightly gets the applause, it has its own limits, so the most effective way most people have of helping others is to do the best they can at the service or producing the product they do and that others desire and are willing to pay for. This is nothing fancier than "working", and if you do your job well you are fulfilling yourself and your role in the grand parade. Whether you make millions or just enough for yourself and family carries no greater or less moral distinction. This is an unrecognized, necessary implication of the "invisible hand".

And self interest in economics is far broader than the common misimpression allows. We are all human beings with a broad range of beliefs, affinities, interests, and connections. We have many different ways we seek to spend our time, energy, or money. Therefore, as Milton Friedman explained, "self interest" in economics is not the cardboard character of ridicule usually depicted, but includes:

> "the whole range of values men hold dear and for which they are willing to spend their fortunes and sacrifice their lives. ...It is the virtue of a free society that it nevertheless permits [charitable, educational, religious, etc.] interests free scope and does not subordinate them to the narrow materialistic interests that dominate the bulk of mankind. That is why capitalist societies are less materialistic than collectivist societies."[2]

Much of the hostility to free markets and commercial life arises from ignorance or confusion as to these simple ideas.

[1] Adam Smith, *An Inquiry into the Nature and Causes of the Wealth of Nations*, Book IV, Ch. 11 at p 477-8 (U. Chicago Press 1977). See further explanation in Field, *The Bumbling Colossus* at 162, 145-190. Recent work explaining the morality of markets vs the morality of families and tribes is at www.thebumblingcolossus.com, especially the work of Dwight Lee. Public choice is described at William Shughart

II, "Public Choice", in *The Concise Encyclopedia of Economics, Library of Economics and Liberty,* www.econlib.org.

[2] Milton Friedman, *Capitalism and Freedom,* at 200–201 (U. Chicago Press 1962). Discussion of dual morality thanks to Dwight Lee, "Moderating the Dark Side of Emotional Morality", *The Independent Review,* vol 17 at 209 (2012)). Also J. R. Clark & Dwight R. Lee, "Markets and Morality", 31 *Cato Journal,* No. 1 (2011). Friedman received the Nobel Prize in Economics in 1976, Stigler in 1982, Hayek in 1974, Buchanan in 1986, and Coase in 1991.

9

Why Health Care is Not a "Market Failure"

9. Looking at Health Care as a "Market Failure" is a Harmful Fallacy

The economic justification of government intervention in markets "usually rests on a claim of 'market failure'". [1] This theory allows its proponents to disregard known market benefits, substituting schemes of government control. And indeed, "market failure" is just what the advocates of government controlled health care argue.[2] The academic support for this, always thin, has been long demolished.

The intellectual case for health care as a market failure requiring or justifying government intervention was made by Ken Arrow, a Professor of Economics who received a Nobel Prize for other work, in a 1963 article.[3] He differentiated health care from other markets on the basis of five features: unpredictable needs and demands, licenses to practice creating barriers to entry, the trust relationship of doctor and patient, asymmetrical information (doctor knows more than patient), and lack of cost transparency. Since under ideal market conditions these five factors are not present, he concluded a case exists for government intervention to regulate relations. Following his lead, over time our health care system has seen ever greater government intervention.

But these five factors are in no way unique to health care and, in fact, most markets operate with many of them while competition allows prices to decline and products improve as providers strive to fill wants. Few markets have predictable demand, but thrive free of government controls. Many industries have economic or technology barriers limiting entry, but prices respond to competition, without government. Trust is a factor in most markets, but that doesn't stop transactions from flourishing, without government interference. Insurers ferret out remote areas of care to price risk regardless of price transparency.[4]

Moreover, Singapore's highly successful experience with a market-based health care system, initiated after Arrow's 1963 piece, clearly demonstrates that his market failure theory, welcome as it was to progressives, lacked real-world verisimilitude and could not survive outside the classroom.

Arrow's analysis also rests on a critical logical flaw. He contrasts existing health care conditions with an intellectual ideal. This is an example of what noted economist Harold Demsetz calls "the nirvana approach", where failure is always found because rarely do existing conditions meet the ideal of perfect market competition. Instead, the comparison should be between two real situations, what he called "the comparative institutional approach":

> "The nirvana approach is much more susceptible than is the comparative institutional approach to committing three logical fallacies – *the grass is always greener fallacy,* the *fallacy of the free lunch*, and the *people could be different fallacy*."[5]

All three fallacies feature in Arrow's analysis of health care as a "market failure". Because by definition conditions in an ideal state are optimal, any contrast with a real market will result in the "grass being greener" in the ideal or the unexamined alternative. Because none of the costs of government intervention — both compliance costs and the costs of lost growth and competitiveness (which are huge) — are part of the analysis, it falsely assumes that government intervention is without cost at all – the "free lunch fallacy". Then, as a last resort, advocates of government control argue that to make it work human nature can be changed, for the better, with proper instruction and modeling by bureaucracies – the "people could be different fallacy". Good luck there.

These fallacies have found home in old progressive thinking. The constant impulse to reach for a new government regulation or agency to "cure" every problem is a standard feature of the old progressive program. The unexamined alternative always beckons. But repetition and agitation do not make a failed approach somehow better. And this failure is no longer news. Years ago, the great Nobel Prize economist George Stigler summed it up:

> "In truth, I consider both the complex theory of welfare economics – for that is what we call the economic analysis of market failures – and that blend of hope and cynicism which passes for political wisdom, to have been infertile and obfuscatory."[6]

Not just "infertile and obfuscatory", but dead wrong. A recent careful, wide-ranging study directly tested Arrow's thesis, noting that despite a lack of research supporting it:

> "...for decades, experts and policy wonks have argued that health care is a uniquely inefficient industry, insulated from conventional market forces that operate in the rest of the economy. Patients are believed to be uninformed about hospital quality, insurance reduces the incentives to shop for better deals, and government programs aren't sufficiently responsive to quality."

The study noted that if this were true, patients would not choose better from worse among providers. They would not create demand for higher-performing hospitals, nor pressure lower-performing ones to improve, nor respond to outcomes. So the study examined hospitals in various regions, by quality rank, market share changes, health outcomes, and other relevant factors.

What did the study show? Conducted by four Professors of Economics and Health Policy with endowed chairs at Chicago, Harvard, MIT and Columbia, they found that:

> "market forces operate in health care with surprising consistency and impact. ...patients are not simply pawns when receiving medical care" but "exercise the ability to place demand-side pressure on care providers.... even for emergency conditions."

> "Contrary to conventional wisdom that the health care sector is insulated from consumer pressures, the opposite is largely true. It means that efforts that strengthen these forces may be beneficial to patients. ... Our finding that demand is a key force in influencing outcomes in the health sector means it is important to ensure that patients have the ability to make express choices."

The principal investigators were Professors Chandra, Finkelstein, Secarny & Syverson, and the *Harvard Business Review* published it under the title: "Research: Perhaps Market Forces Do Work in Health Care After All" (12/05/2016 edition), adding the wry tagline, "Now they tell us."

Indeed. But no one needed to await the outcome of this study. Just look at the real life experience of Singapore's health system. It is long past time to reject the ObamaCare approach and return to encouraging the free market, where patients can exercise choice, insurers are free to shape policies to meet discrete demands and cost preferences, and providers compete for patient attention.

Although Arrow's analysis of health care as a "market failure" has been thoroughly refuted in theory, studies, and real world experience, that does not stop the dogged old progressive from continuing to flog its flawed results. Paul Krugman of the N. Y. Times, for example, still cites and relies on Arrow's paper in advocating his numerous prescriptions for government intervention in health and many other fields.

[1] *Market Failure or Success: The New Debate*, by Tyler Cowen & Eric

Crampton, at 3 (Edward Elgar & Independent Institute 2002)(shows how modern theories of inefficiency, network effects, asymmetry, and the like have not proved fertile support for "market failure").

[2] See, e.g., Theodore Marmor, "Market Failure", *The Washington Monthly*, April 2000. Yale Professor Marmor is a leading advocate of a single-payer system.

[3] Kenneth Arrow, "Uncertainty and the Welfare Economics of Medical Care" (*American Economic Review*, December 1963).

[4] Avik Roy, "Health Care and the Profit Motive", 3 *National Affairs*, at 40-45 (Spring 2010). Singapore's results, described in chapter 6, confirm the powerful positive effects of a market-based approach to healthcare.

[5] Harold Demsetz, "Information and Efficiency: Another Viewpoint", *The Journal of Law & Economics*, vol. 12 at 1 (1969). On the enormous hidden costs and burdens of regulation, read the federal government's own SBA report, "The Impact of Regulatory Costs on Small Firms", Nicole V. and W. Mark Crain, Lafayette College (Sept. 2010)(federal regulations cost the equivalent of 14% of national income, half again all expenditures for health care, disproportionately harming small firms), quoted and discussed in Field, *The Bumbling Colossus,* at 182-6 (2012).

[6] George J. Stigler, "The Economists' Traditional Theory of the Economic Functions of the State", in *The Citizen and the State; Essays on Regulation*, at 103 (U. Chicago Press 1975).

10

Support Participation, Don't Cripple the Beast

10. Carefully Designed Support Enhances Beneficial Market Forces

Markets exist to provide people with the ability to transact for what they want. Not all people participate in particular markets, for various reasons. Now comes the health care market, and political forces decree that everyone should participate regardless of whether they can afford to do so. This is not market failure. This is government seeking to expand the participants in a functioning market (not that today's health care system rife with government controls is really functioning).

There is nothing wrong with this. But listen. It makes a huge difference whether you say, "Health care is not a functioning market at all, it is a market failure", or whether you say, "Let's supplement the market so all can participate". In the first case, your thinking leads to government intervention or takeover. In the second, you think of how to subsidize those outside the market so they can participate. The first gives you near-total control by regulation or government ownership, effected via enormous top-down bureaucracies. The second avoids bureaucracy and sends money (credits, vouchers in HSAs) directly to the people who need it so they can make their own choices. The benefits of the second are what we explain here.

Too often, liberals and progressives excoriate free market proponents as "mean spirited", unwilling to aid those who need it. This is untrue and unhelpful. There is nothing in free market principles which says government should not lend a helping hand where needed. The problem is not support carefully designed to avoid dependency, but the creation of special privileges, through intrusive regulation and control. Long ago free market proponent F.A. Hayek said:

> "Let a uniform minimum be secured to everybody by all means, but let us admit at the same time that with this assurance of a basic minimum all claims for a privileged security of particular classes must lapse, that all excuses disappear for allowing groups to exclude newcomers from sharing their relative prosperity in order to maintain a special standard of their own." (*The Road to Serfdom*, at 210 (1944).

Of course subsidy where unnecessary and not carefully tailored creates its own dangers, pulling people into on-going poverty instead of helping them out of it. ObamaCare went too far in its support of those well above the poverty line. A large deliberate first step towards socialized medicine. It created a new middle class entitlement, creating dependency, which is enormously difficult to take away.

In addition to creating a large political constituency resisting change, extending new benefits creates additional demand for services. This requires expanding supply — more doctors, hospitals, nurses, etc. This need is minimized here, however, as we have already provided subsidy for the poor and near-poor under current arrangements (ObamaCare subsidizes well above the poverty line). So the impact of the HSA credit/voucher regime set out here on demand should be minimal, possibly even reducing it from current levels if public support is limited, as it should be, to the genuine poor or near poor. The primary impact of the HSA approach is to reduce the cost trajectory by resting the system on personal and family responsibility in active free markets.

11

Wash those Dead Ideas Right Out of Your Hair

11. The Myth that Free Markets Foster Greed and Harm the Public

Many people giving lip service to, or disparaging free markets believe they foster greed and other vices which harm others. Arenas for "the rich" to prey on others. This is common to hear from the pulpit, although ironically the money supporting these people comes from the private sector. Academics are also unusually susceptible to this belief.

This complaint arises from a basic confusion. Commercial life depends on trust and reliability. Sure, there are exceptions, but those usually are quickly found out. A lying businessman soon finds his customers going elsewhere. The market is not like a wildebeest feasted upon by lions, where the strong eat their fill at the expense of the weak. In free markets, it is the opposite. Bread costs the same whether you are a millionaire or pauper. Each person is free to contribute their skill or capital according to their desire. Each person orders their preferences according to their taste.

The question always is, what can you add, that people want to pay you for? Not, how much wildebeest can you eat at the expense of a weaker lion. I don't impoverish anyone by my consumption. The market is built upon voluntary, win-win transactions; hence, Adam Smith's Paradox, where the individual pursuing his own interest benefits the larger society.

As suggested above, what people miss is that commercial life fosters virtues we all take for granted. As Yuval Levin points out:

> "Market players have a powerful incentive to consider what others will think of their actions, since they have to appeal to those others as customers. And the virtues most valued in sellers and buyers are precisely [Adam] Smith's moderate virtues: prudence and thrift, honesty and reliability, civility and good order – in short, again: discipline. The market, as Smith saw it, is a powerful tool of discipline. It demands and rewards habits of peaceful order, and can spread these into the larger society."[1]

After eight years where government intervention has been touted at the highest levels and echoed by media and the broad professoriat, and markets denigrated as inadequate and ruinous (especially falsely blamed for bringing on the Great Recession of 2007-08), it is important once again to return to fundamentals. The blaming of that implosion on markets – corporate greed, loose regulation, derivatives run amok, and the like – was a superficial and erroneous call. Instead, as now has become amply clear, it was not the free market system which was the precipitating cause of the collapse, but government intervention run amok in the housing markets.

[1] Yuval Levin, "Recovering the Case for Capitalism", 3 *National Affairs*, at 127 (Spring 2010). The virtues described are in Adam Smith, *The Theory of Moral Sentiments*, London 1754).

12

The 2007–08 Crisis: How Public Agents Spurred it On, then Hid

12. A Ship of Fools; Government Created the Crisis and Blamed the Market

The markets got the blame for the 2007–08 Great Recession while the government actors who, over the prior decades, had laid the wood on the fire and touched the match saved their scalps and scapegoated others. The impetus, as so often is the case, was a well-motivated, idealistic desire by old progressive politicians, led in the Senate by Chris Dodd of Connecticut and in the House by Barney Frank of Massachusetts, to increase home ownership among the poor. They were convinced that housing finance was a market failure which left many deserving people on the sidelines. So they pressured for federal financial regulators to accept ever lower standards for home loans.

This was accomplished from the early 1990s on through HUD's "Best Practices Initiative", Fannie Mae and Freddie Mac's ever expanded purchases of ever worse credits, the Community Reinvestment Act (which allowed local groups to contest bank mergers and efforts to expand), and consistent vocal Congressional push (mainly by Dodd and Frank taking the high moral ground) to force lower and lower mortgage standards so those unable to afford homes could nonetheless buy them. Cowed, the others (of both parties) followed.

This idealistic but short-sighted effort was carried on through the Clinton, Bush and Obama administrations, the last even after the crash and after the true cause had been "outed".[1] While it was going on, the moral posturing of those creating the "thought framework" made it impossible to stop. Nobody wanted to be seen as heartless. Everyone believed what the N.Y. Times and the dominant media put out on behalf of the political originators of the crisis. To boot, President Clinton had famously promised at the inception that the whole thing, being off the federal books, would "not cost the taxpayer one red cent". The government was just pressuring the private actors, primarily by regulation lowering housing lending standards. This is what I call in *The Bumbling Colossus* "the Regulatory Illusion" – belief in the cost-free limitation of the market. Nonetheless, as we all can now recount, the result was a financial and human disaster of the first proportions.

Afterward, the "thought framework" continued. Because the dominant political and media sources, repeating their old learned narrative, once again sought to blame private actors and the market, not the government interventions, most people still remain ignorant of what really drove the catastrophe. The blindness, once fixed, became hard to modify.

In truth, as has been amply shown, the private markets were followers and amplifiers, not causers.[2] Peter J. Wallison has written the definitive comprehensive analysis, which concludes:

> "The preceding chapters showed that government housing policy, implemented principally by HUD through Fannie Mae and Freddie Mac, reduced mortgage underwriting standards, built an unprecedented housing bubble, and – in combination with mark-to-market accounting and a blundering government response – was the principal cause of the 2008 financial crisis. Thus, the conventional narrative about the crisis – that it was caused by lax government regulation of private financial institutions – is false." ....

> "If the public believes that the financial crisis was caused by insufficient regulation of the financial sector, and that the housing policies of government pursued between 1992 and 2008 had no role in the events of 2007 and 2008, a return of the same faulty

policies are inevitable in the future. The real lesson of the financial
crisis will not have been learned."

To really move on in a helpful manner, this truth must be confronted
and admitted by the old progressives and their liberal followers who
proudly took the lead in degrading market standards and thereby
wreaking the harms.

[1] Raghuram G. Rajan, *Fault Lines: How Hidden Fractures Still Threaten
the World Economy*, Ch. 1, "Let Them Eat Credit" (Princeton U. Press
2010)(former chief economist, World Bank). See also generally, Field,
The Bumbling Colossus, at 10-26, 201-210.

[2] Peter J. Wallison, *Hidden in Plain Sight; What Really Caused the
World's Worst Financial Crisis and Why It Could Happen Again*, at 342,
350 (Encounter Books 2015). See also Peter J. Wallison, *Dissent to
Report of the Financial Crisis Inquiry Commission* (2011); Professor
Charles W. Calomiris, "The Mortgage Crisis: Some Inside Views",
10/27/2011 *WSJ;* Calomiris & Haber, *Fragile by Design; The Political
Origins of Banking Crises and Scarce Credit,* at 256-83 (Princeton 2014).

13

Greed: Public and Private Contrasted

13. How Government Intervention Enables Privilege and Greed

Greed is an easy but unhelpful strike against markets. Of course greed exists and creates harms. But this is true in all endeavors, including the non-profit, the religious, the socialist, the public interest organizations, government, academia. But notice the difference: only in competitive commercial life is there a self-correction mechanism keeping greed in check. Mistreat customers, lower your quality or unreasonably raise your price, and they go elsewhere.

Greed is more a slur against others than a clear-cut phenomenon. Its definition is labile. My worthy reward is your greedy excess. And everywhere it is scorned and where illegal, proscribed — as in laws which prohibit taking advantage of others, as in breaches of trust, stealing, fraud, misrepresentation, and the like.

The market entrepreneur displays the opposite of greed: discipline, frugality, creativity, energy, self-denial. Greed is getting something for nothing. Something for nothing more closely tracks the kind of activity one sees where government has intervened in markets. In government regulated industries, bureaucrats are placed in positions to lend favors and allow benefits to accrue to favored insiders or powerful interests. Politically elevated actors in government and their beneficiaries outside achieve their positions not by serving others in voluntary transactions, as in free market commerce, but by laws, regulations, tariffs, subsidies, or some form of political advancement which allow favors and enable special rewards. In the economic literature and discussion, this non-market system of extraction is called "rents". [1]

So those seeking the greedy should re-calibrate their aim. The most obvious source of greed – something for nothing – is not the free market, but those promoting and taking advantage of public regulations, rules and enactments — always promoted and clothed in misleading claims of the public interest to mollify the politically naive — which actually result in discriminatory protections harboring and enriching a few.

"Crony capitalism" is an obvious and legitimate candidate for No. 1 on the list of greed-inducing activities or rents. This is where government and select private interests combine for mutual nest-feathering. Instead of having to compete in the open market, these select private interests, protected by publicly approved laws, regs, and their bureaucratic and political administrators, use their "legitimate" perch to exclude others from competing, allow monopoly pricing, promote and maintain subsidy, create regulatory burdens for others, and otherwise perpetuate their privilege. Regulation, tariffs, and subsidy are the tools of choice.

Unlike temporary monopolies in free market economies, usually the result of technology advances, crony capitalism is extremely hard to dislodge.[2] In this country, this unhappy situation is a principal unfortunate side-effect of intrusive industry regulation. It is pervasive, a feature of virtually all regulatory schemes. Usually the large players capture the legislators and the regulators, and make sure the regulatory language and interpretation is crafted to their ends. The courts aid this by "judicial deference" to administrative interpretation and discretion. Protected enclaves are created and persist. The high public purposes get lost. This is so pronounced, as explained before, it even has a name, "regulatory capture".

Latin America, Russia, and many other countries also more visibly display this problem, where political elites control business and visa-versa and continue indefinitely their protected positions. Seeing this in another country is easy, but for some reason the blinders go on at home. People are too easily seduced by self interest masquerading as the "public interest".

Crony Capitalism is the opposite of a free market. It is a market of restricted entry and less than fully competitive pricing to the detriment of the consumer and the public. A strong argument against intrusive regulation. Adam Smith saw this years ago and it remains true. Free markets, despite bad press from poorly educated old progressives and their media/political cohorts, benefit ordinary people far better than any known alternative. That is where the future lies.

[1] Gordon Tullock described and elaborated this phenomenon. See David R. Henderson, "Rent Seeking", *The Concise Encyclopedia of Economics*, www.econlib.org. For discussion of the distinction between "market entrepreneurs" who gain share by efficiency and low pricing vs. "political entrepreneurs" who gain share by obtaining political advantages allowing them to raise prices, and examples of each, see Burton W. Folsom, Jr., *The Myth of the Robber Barons: A New Look at the Rise of Big Business in America* (7th ed 2013). A more recent example of rents is The Clinton Foundation, whose assets have swollen to the hundreds of millions while Hillary Clinton was Senator, Secretary of State, and Presidential candidate.

[2] George J. Stigler, "The Economic Effects of the Antitrust Laws", in *The Organization of Industry* (U. Chicago Press 1968). Stigler, Milton Friedman, Aaron Director, and others — following the lead of Adam Smith two centuries before — led the revolution against intrusive regulation, its political cover stories, and unjustified privileges which forms the bedrock of economic analysis today.

14

Public Sector Unions and Private: Beware the Rent-Seekers

14. Rent Seeking at Our Expense by Public Sector Unions and Private

Old progressives looked at private sector labor unions as foundations for policy and politics. They were of uncertain legal status until the Wagner Act of 1935, because monopolizing labor ran afoul of state and federal laws as a conspiracy in restraint of trade. Becoming a legal monopoly helped them to improve working conditions and pay in some industries over time, and gave political voice to many. But unions increase wages and improve conditions for only their own. By raising production costs, they serve to reduce demand for labor, reduce jobs, and make life harder for those outside seeking work. Even for many of those union members who thought they would be benefited. There's no free lunch, even at the corporate table. A principal reason for industrial decline where unions are entrenched. An unhappy side effect of having fewer jobs available — unions' long history as bastions of discrimination.

For numerous reasons, we have seen declining interest in private sector unions – their percentage in the work force reached an all-time low in 2016, even though the Obama administration promoted union "card check" and similar pro-union policies on the benighted theory that increasing their scope and power would somehow benefit the rest of society.

Unions in the public sector are another story. Police, fire, teachers, emergency responders, bureaucrats, and other persons employed by government were not covered by the 1935 Wagner Act allowing private unions. They were not allowed to form unions (except postal workers) at the state or federal level, with the exception of NYC and Wisconsin, until JFK allowed them by executive order in 1962. Previously, it was considered wrong for government workers to strike or bring similar pressure on political managers, for not the least of reasons that those managers, unlike managers in private industry, lacked a financial stake in opposing them. It is too easy to cave in to demands when the cost is borne only by a remote public unable to sort out the increase among all the influences in general tax rates. This remains true. Public unions are a paradigmatic example of a system of rents.

Perhaps for this very reason, public employees have joined public sector unions in increasing record numbers, quite unlike their counterparts in private industry. They understand the special benefit rents afford. The fact remains, nonetheless, that there is a basic immorality underlying this phenomenon, even apart from rents. This was expressed by FDR as follows:

> "All Government employees should realize that the process of collective bargaining, as usually understood, can not be transplanted into the public service. ...The employer is the whole people, who speak by means of laws enacted by their representatives in Congress. ...Since their own services have to do with the functioning of the Government, a strike of public employees manifests nothing less than an intent on their part to prevent or obstruct the operations of Government until their demands are satisfied. Such action, looking toward the paralysis of Government by those who have sworn to support it, is unthinkable and intolerable."[1]

Now these public sector unions form a formidable political force demanding the attention of politicians, especially the Democratic Party, which has become known as "the party of the public sector unions."

Politically expedient, this formidable political base is unhealthy for the party which depends upon it. For example, the teachers' union has come to be viewed as an agent for the self-interest of teachers and opposed to that of students and parents. Their monolithic rejection of charter schools, school vouchers and similar efforts to enrich the education of especially minority inner-city children, regardless of the strong evidence that such alternative schools substantially benefit particularly the inner-city poor, has gained adverse attention.[2] Unlike the local Alabama prosecutor in the great legal comedy "My Cousin Vinny", they don't seem to "welcome the competition".

Having a giant political army in the government sector is harmful to society in other ways. It provides a constant pressure to expand government; More agencies, larger programs, increased budgets – all flow from the push/pull this huge pressure group provides. Politicians captured by this demographic insist not only on new and bigger government agencies and programs, with more and more people becoming dependent on government largesse, but that these new programs (e.g., Transportation Security, Dodd-Frank) be staffed with government rather than private hires. Whether the job is equally or better done by the private sector, or with non-government workers is not examined. Ever-expanding government is the result, until a vicious cycle kicks in, where politicians create more grateful voters who – dependent on government – vote for them, the public sector swells unimaginably, growth of the private sector slows, private sector jobs shrink, dependency replaces an independent spirit, and the stultifying world of a kind of near-socialism decay settles in over what was once the greatest economic powerhouse in the world.

This is ultimately self-defeating, as surveys of socialism around the world clearly reveal.[3] This is not a future Americans can look forward to, and the liberal and New Progressive recognize in this the nightmare which spells political defeat as well. Better to now seize the day. The New Progressive/liberal sees the virtue of competition in business and education, cuts the cords of affinity with the public sector unions which insist on self-aggrandizing at all cost, and takes the lead in promoting America's best interests as well.

[1] Franklin D. Roosevelt, "Letter on the Resolution of Federation of Federal Employees Against Strikes in Federal Service", *Presidency.ucsb.edu*. On employees and unions benefiting from discrimination, see Gary S. Becker, *The Economics of Discrimination* at 13-14 (Chicago 1957).

[2] See, e.g., Peterson, Henderson & West, *Teachers versus the Public – What Americans Think about Schools and How to Fix Them*, (Brookings Institution Press 2014). Paul E. Peterson, Shattuck Professor of Government at Harvard and his two associates demonstrate by careful statistics and surveys, the enormous gap between teacher attitudes against change and competition, and public recognition of the damage to students this attitude entails.

[3] See, e.g., Joshua Muravchik, *Heaven on Earth: The Rise and Fall of Socialism* (Encounter Books 2002), which describes the universal catastrophe socialism brings. Venezuela is a tragic current example. A basic source is Milton Friedman, *Capitalism and Freedom* (U. Chicago 1962). The theoretical nonsense socialism creates is spelled out in Stigler, George J., *Essays in the History of Economics*, (U. Chicago 1965) at 268 et seq., and Thomas Sowell, *Marxism: Philosophy and Economics* (Quill, William Morrow 1985)("the Marxian contribution to economics can readily be summarized as virtually zero. ... however historic it may be as the centerpiece of a worldwide political movement.").

15

The Merger of the New Progressives and Liberal Conservatism

15. The Merger of the New Progressive and Liberal Conservatism

The astute reader will have noticed how closely convergent the new progressive approach is to a kind of generous conservative political economy. For example, the health care approach sketched above is based on well-established, sound, tested economics, normally the domain of conservatives, but expanded to embrace the progressive ideals of universality and affordable access. In this way what have traditionally been sworn enemies and fodder for political rancor are suddenly seen to stand together for the same practical program. As if by magic, war transmutes into peace, dedicated enemies into soul mates, extreme rhetoric into kind words. Much is gained.

About the Author:

Henry F. Field is a graduate of Harvard College and the University of Chicago Law School. He studied under Aaron Director, "The Father of Law and Economics", and was Special Assistant to Edward H. Levi, President of the University of Chicago. He knew, and read extensively the works of, major economists at the top of the field, including many Nobel Prize winners. The harvest of much of that appears here and in the works described. He is an "amateur" in the old-fashioned sense — a lover of knowledge. He translates complex and often esoteric material so the ordinary interested reader can enjoy and understand.

He practiced law and has published in major legal journals and in the public arena. His website is **www.thebumblingcolossus.com**. This is where you go for recent significant developments in the topics discussed here and in his recent book, *The Bumbling Colossus* (amazon.com 2012).

He is a Life Member of the American Law Institute, and listed in *Who's Who in America,* 1980.

He has always been a political independent, although he worked to support the political campaigns of Rep. Abner Mikva and Senator Hubert Humphrey.

He lives in Massachusetts with his wonderful wife and his American Eskimo, Dorje. His children are grown and independent, and his grandson, about to be so.

www.ingramcontent.com/pod-product-compliance
Lightning Source LLC
Chambersburg PA
CBHW032153020426
42334CB00016B/1269